A Mandala Coloring Book For Adults
MANDALA
Flower Patterns
Coloring Book
I0758915

Written & Illustrated by:
Bling King Publishing

www.ingramcontent.com/pod-product-compliance
Lightning Source LLC
Chambersburg PA
CBHW080224260726
48658CB00008B/2997